Imperfect Echoes

Writing Truth and Justice with Capital Letters, lie and oppression with Small

By Carolyn Howard-Johnson

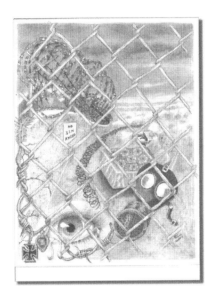

HowToDoItFrugally Publishing
Los Angeles, CA

Trademarks and myriad names of products, journals, and businesses used in this work are not authorized by, associated with, or sponsored by the trademark owners. No association with the corporations or names is implied or intended.

ISBN-13:978-1515232490
ISBN-10:1515232492

Art by Richard Conway Jackson ©.
Carolyn's headshot by Uriah Carr.
Logo by Lloyd King.

Printed in the United States of America.

This book is available at a discount when purchased in quantity to use as premiums, sales promotions, in corporate training programs, or by schools or social organizations for educational purposes. For information, please contact the author at HoJoNews@aol.com.

Poets don't discard disaster;
they thrive on it.
~ Carolyn Howard-Johnson

Way back in 1953 when I was beginning to pay attention to Nobel laureates, Czeslaw Milosz published a book called *The Captive Mind.* The *Los Angeles Times* called Milosz's book an "unmatched account of the evils attendant on intellectual accommodation to political expediency." Here is an excerpt from the poem "Incantation" in that book.

"Human reason is beautiful and invincible.
No bars, no barbed wire, no pulping of books,
No sentence of banishment can prevail against it.
It establishes the universal ideas in language,
And guides our hand so we write Truth and Justice
With capital letters, lie and oppression with small."

Milosz's words makes us wonder why—so many years later—the world is not focusing on lovely words like Peace, Tolerance, Hope, Truth, Justice, and Acceptance. Poets are forgetting to capitalize them, but remembering to give that honor to the names of wars.

Proceeds from this book will be donated to
Amnesty International.

To remember is to relive; to relive is to survive beyond tomorrow.
~ Carolyn Howard-Johnson

Human Reason requires
remembering mistakes, accepting
an uncomfortable now for the
betterment of the future.
~ Carolyn Howard-Johnson

Acknowledgements

It is a lovely tradition in the world of poetry to list those who have previously published poems selected for a new collection. This is just such an almanac—with my gratitude—of poems that have appeared in other books, chapbooks, anthologies, and journals.

"The War Museum at Oslo" and "Everywhere My Dream" from *Tracings*, a chapbook published by Finishing Line Press.

"Olvera Street Tutorial" published in *The Pedestal Magazine* and winner of their first readers' choice award. Edited by John Amen.

"Crying Walls" published as "Inevitably Walls" in *Solo Novo 2011: Wall Scrawls*.

"Peril" published in *Copperfield Review*.

"déjà vu" published in *Barricade*. Edited by John Newmark.

"Antigua's Hope" published by *Penwomanship*.

"Perfectly Flawed" published in *The Journal of the Image Warehouse*.

"Earliest Remembered Sound" published in *Apollos Lyre*.

"Whiling Summer's Hours" published in *Long Story Short*.

"Ypres' Jewish Grave"
published by *Cyclamen and Swords.*

"Utah's Song" from *This Is the Place.*

"St. Petersburg Sestina"
from *Copperfield Review.*

"Death by Ferris Wheel"
published by *Pear Noir.*

"Sacred Stories of the Sierras" published
by *Manzanita Literary Journal,*
associated with Calaveras Arts Council.

**Poems from The Celebration Series
of chapbooks by
Magdalena Ball and
Carolyn Howard-Johnson**

"Narcissus Revisited"
from *Deeper Into the Pond.*

"From the Observation Deck"
from *Cherished Pulse.*

"The Giraffe"
from *Sublime Planet.*

"Sifting Out Life's Dregs"
from *She Wore Emerald Then.*

Imperfect Echoes

Writing Truth and Justice with Capital Letters, lie and oppression with Small

By Carolyn Howard-Johnson

Illustrations by
Richard Conway Jackson

Prologue

Apologies from a Magpie

My mentor opines
What can possibly be said
about war that has not been said before.

I, a magpie,
tell her *said before*
has not done the job.
Black ink here, white
there (no gray or silver nuances).
The future fears
blank pages.
I fear silence
more than censure.
So what if my obvious colors
shine like snowflake
obsidian in sunshine.
So what if my melody
has been sung by others.
Magpies are born to sing others' songs—
stained notes, imperfect echoes—
until the world begins to know
them by heart.

Contents

ACCEPTANCE: WAITING FOR THE GIFT 69

Remembering What We Must

"My uncle's souvenirs laid out on a chenille spread. A Glock. A green iron cross. A canteen in a canvas pouch. His own Purple Heart."

It's in the Knowing

I want to know. . .
how my marrow
ran in their bones. If these Cycladic figures
inspired Picasso, flat-faced; Miro,
expressionless. But Quakers
who stitched sunbonnet girls
on quilts knew Keros not at all,
nor farmers and fishers,
nor those who pillaged their ancient
shards. Mayans pulled faceless dolls
from husks of corn, never knew this one,
broken arm, vagina visible
between its open legs, harp in its lap. Still
it music melts over five millenniums
to touch me,
allow me to put
my face on its.

Crying Walls

Near Jerusalem, razorwire
coils a brutal line

imposed like walls
Lennon imagined

might one day disappear.
This one much like the first wall

I unexpectedly came across somewhere
in memory, an ocean away

marking its territory
East from West, the wall

that called my husband to arms,
just in case. Another wall,

cleaves Irish from Irish. Foreign
walls, but now a new one

crawls from Baja,
through mountain passes

along the Rio Grande. Walls.
Chains-linked. Wire-barbed,

Krylon-smeared. Feeble,
useless, unholy billboards,

anything but mending walls.

Drumbeat

WWI, WWII, Korea, Bosnia, Kosovo, First
Gulf War, War on Terror, Ukraine, Berlin
Crisis, Afghanistan, Kuwait, Bay of Pigs,
Desert Storm, Libya, Rwanda, Iraq (one
and two). Words like a drum's bass
beat. One lifetime, decades of wars
to remember, losing track
of names, I with no idea
if remembering makes
things better
or worse.

Earliest Remembered Sound

All the sound in the world sucked
to one wavering, wailing note
I perch on my father's knee,
afraid, look through our window
Utah's lights snuff, quickly, quickly,
silver sequins turn dark
until the skyline disappears
against deep black silk. There,
among our overstuffed chairs
where doilies protect fat rolled arms.
The siren whines to silence.

What could that have been?

Oh, nothing, an air raid
my mother answers
as if her words were lyrics
she wanted to forget.
Would the lights return
charged with that sound that split
my father's hand from mine.
Father wears a cunt cap, grosgrain ribbons
across his heart; smells of gabardine
and good-byes. His eyelids twitch.
Mother once again says,

Oh, probably nothing at all.

St. Petersburg Sestina

**Upon my visit to *Peskaryovskoye Kladbishe* in 2002
sixty years after Tanya Savachev wrote her brief eulogies.**

Shards of diary left
behind by Russia's Ann Frank. Yellow-dyed
pages torn from her notebook since the time
of this city's sorrow, 1942,
silent cemetery, eternal mounds. Only
inscriptions from her hand cry

to visitors who, in their turn, try not to cry
try not to blur the messages she left.
By '41 Zhenya gone. Not only
Zhenya but Babushka and Erena died
in that winter's siege, 1941,
Leningrad's longest, bitterest time

when life was not long enough. Time
counted by deaths. Tanya cried
with her pen. Three dead by March of '42.
Each death a page. Uncle Vasya left.
One page more. *Mamma died.*
May 13th. 1942. 7:30 a.m. Only

then did Tanya's Cyrillic falter, only
a bit. Behind the blockade. May promises time,
tulips, an easier life. Winter had died.
Survival allows no time to laugh, no time to cry.
Sieges know no season. Tanya took what was left.
What was left in the spring of 1942

Continued

was bodies. Tanya's entry of 1942—
May 10th —she wrote *Uncle Losha.* Only
his name, date of death, left
here. Remnants left for this time.
Next, frail, her words cry
The Savachevs have all died,

no date or time—no need. All have died,
absent evidence. Despair of '42.
Tanya's silent cry,
memoir on mortal scraps. Only
The Savachev's have all died, Times
gone, everyone gone. *Only Tanya is left.*

This Klabishe journal, cryptic text left to curl and die
after Tanya's time, the mourning of 1942,
leaves only the city's seagulls to cry. Aloud.

Visit to Kirovsk

On the occasion of my visit to the Russian monument commemorating the siege of Leningrad.

To commemorate what happened here, bronze erupts from a slope slanting from the highway to the Neva. A tonsure surrounds its thrust, bald land circled by summer's sod, trampled, evidence of those who stop along the way to Staraya Ladoga.

This artery led the Nazis to Leningrad, opened itself a spliced vein onto those behind its battlements. Numb. Soldiers fertilized it here with relics, pocked the path with remnants of their siege.

My uncle's souvenirs laid out on a chenille spread. A Glock. A green iron cross. A canteen in a canvas pouch. His own Purple Heart.

A breeze from the river evaporates memories. At the monument's base rusty memorial bouquets. This helmet. That blade. An exhausted hose, corrugated like a windpipe. Here a mask; huge grasshopper head, mandibles, vacant eyes. They tarnish there. No one here thinks to carry them home.

Awful Splendor

My screen, seldom used
I wipe away a frail skin,
dust, residual surface calm.
I don't watch TV, I say, *but* . . .
I search unfamiliar contours
to find the power icon. Click.
The dark panel flickers.
A flame coils from the desert,
floor, a tornado from Hades,
desert dancers costumed
in orange-hot veils.
I do not turn up the sound.
A mute portrait, framed. An image
on a museum wall seen by
night's camera-eyes as green
fluorescent bursts against a
sky the color of Wedgwood's
Portland blue. A triptych.
Here, a camouflage palette
the colors of geckos skittering
over the sand. There, a Turner,
hazy as if seen through
early morning vapor. And look!
There mauve clouds pulse.
Siroccos blow a purple pall
across the horizon, soundless winds
smear the scene, disguise
it with a mask of splendor.

The Digital World as Metaphor

"Love letters in the sand."
Time-Life's lasers, magic

borealis mirrors, carry-about jewels
in shock-pockets clear

as distilled dew. Shaman discs
thunder, *"Ghost Riders in the Sky"*

tinkle *"Mr. Sandman."*
I read, not conscious of verse

or voice until a catch, unexpected,
reminds me of black Frisbee saucers

I kept safe in paper pockets
and still they stuttered from blunted

needles, neighbors thumping
the ceiling, something heavy

in the next room falling.
"Where have all the young men gone . . ."

New technology mimics its ancestors.
"young men, -y-young men, gone . . .

Continued

*to g-graveyards, g-g-graveyards,
g-g-graveyards.*"

The phrase reprised, as if decades
had not passed.

Belgium's Death Fields

Once they said the guns fell
silent but they were wrong.
After that first
numbered war, we saluted,
our own flag, hearts on our sleeves,
the next war the genome for a generation
of storyteller patriots, a few conflicts more
before the war when those troops
who did come home couldn't walk
or wouldn't talk and didn't win. In the wink
of wars ago, the gulf spawned warriors-to-be
who think war is Spic and Span, no dead
on our side, dead on the other untold.
And now a war that takes from the mouths
and hearts of the stranded, the homeless.
How different from those who
marched to snares or flew flags
in a war when we knew
why we were there.

Flanders Fields

Listen, please. We must not forget.
250,000 lost to take a gentle slope.
Somber such a number, they mere echoes

of those whose hearts' liquid fed
these fields long before we counted, kept a toll.
War is our way. Poppies grew there then, grow

there now. No matter how much rot and flies
and fleas, they paint Belgium's pastures
with petals red as blood that soaked

it then. Indomitable spirit, the country builds
itself new these many decades, while other
wars, wildfires, ignite their continent.

We let leaders bludgeon our language,
call them conflicts. They, untruly named,
forgotten. More than one a year after that nearly

forgotten War to End all Wars,
war for Unfathomable Reasons,
our soil paved

with gore,

all our fields poppy-red.

Peril

Nothing is new, peril
persists
in New York's light of early mourning,
invades our arsenals with no warning,
loiters in children's play yard squeals,
in Santee, Selma or Columbine,
in Slavic deathfields,
in Vietnam's slime.
Fanatics destroy a Buddhist retreat;
slaughter soils Zion's bridal suite.
Oklahoma's nursery forever gone
beneath coiled concrete crushed by our own.
Death breathes and whispers
in Lockerbie's mists,
Ruin lies waiting in parking lot decks
for innocence, age, the weaker sex.
Bombs frequent Paris' pretty cafés,
lethal shots stray on Los Angeles' freeways,
Munich's dormitory, Dallas' repository.

We hibernate, shelter our families,
shield our souls.

But wait.

Continued

Peril abides in my night-stand drawer
    gun-metal curled on felt
    like a dormouse sleeping,
    in the hollow of the depressed heart
    that lies in my bed
    and eats from my bowl.
    Does danger lurk
    in the dark of my closet
    or the fist of discipline
    or the noose of justice?

      Where is peace? In the provincial town?
      By my ancestors' primitive campfires?
          Did they not live at risk?

Nothing is new, peril persists.

Apocalypse New

Would the grunt of Viet pigs,
staccato beat of sticks,
chop-chop of blades
hovering low
like deadly mosquitoes,
Saigon ceiling fans,
acid-wet ablution
be hollow gestures
        voices without reason
        unrecognized whispers
        in this dark decade?

Would this millennium recognize
        primordial
        will of the jungle
        as theirs?
                See dank fungus,
                dark spikes of amoral masts
                crucified against slate skies?
                Feel the breath of perfidy?

    I THOUGHT NOT.

Still I curl like an embryonic leaf, unfurled
        on unyielding fired tile,
        a porcelain bowl cool against my palms
        my pursed lids lined with camouflage,

Continued

sliding 's' shapes seen with
borrowed clarity,
thinking how the sun blinds,
hearing the flush of peace.

Perfectly Flawed

Minute by mango colored minute
the sky changes, high clouds whipped
like meringue by astral winds,
the undersides singed by a persimmon
orb settling into the Pacific. I drive
west at 4:30. Saved daylight.
This blush fleeting, in transit.
I should exit at Sepulveda,
pull over to give this display
full attention. Down there, though, among
buildings and trees the view will be reduced
to an overhead tint. The freeway's elevation,
flawed as it is, stokes these fireworks; bumper
threatens bumper, Hondas, SUVs,
battered gardeners' trucks grab
attention from the brilliance
before me. It is 1940. I settle into my uncle's
arms, he on his way to pilot B42s.
Something about the Blitz, something I guess
must be related to lightning, to the undersides
of clouds tinged with fire. He leaves behind
his new Buick, celery colored with peek-a-boo
holes in its side. I, too, soon discarded
to my mother's pale hand. I am required
to make him happy, a child's duty. They don't

Continued

know my blown kiss will be remembered,
stick like early stars to the inverted
sides of a huge aqua glass bowl, that nothing
can be better than the smell of his Barbasol,
his warmth beneath pressed khaki, his breath
sending smoke signals into the twilight.

Rotting Memories

With thanks to Joyce Faulkner,
author of *In the Shadow of Suribachi*

My friend listens
to old men's stories.
Rheumy eyes that
see little else still see
the battle of Dai Do,
not a battle really but
marine-slaughter,
mowed down as they marched
toward a village
as if they had lined up
for a firing squad.

Eddie Beesley lost his legs
at ChuLai in '65, Marvin Snyder
captured, Bill Templeton
a slave laborer. The names
honored for what they endured,
Jim Barnhart, Lloyd King. One,
too overwhelmed with shame
to have his name among them,
was used as trainer for young
captive women who practiced sucking
him through the bars of the cage
they kept him in.

The War Museum at Oslo

Raindrops surf my windshield,
slip across my reflection, tears
not fettered by gravity. I look
into my father's face, decades
gone, rather than my own. Years
later I search for family

seeds. Norway's fjords shed
salty droplets on faces
like my father's. Round faces.
Eyes dilute-blue like the pale
skies above them.
Men who fought

as Churchill's voice crackled
through smuggled vacuum
tubes. Here miniature battles,
cotton snow, charcoaled
clouds, tiny lead replicas of
soldiers now gone, desperate

photo-faces of the condemned. Only days
before I reached this spur, I saw my
grandson off to war, alone.
A sacrifice.

Continued

A trade. For my father
who never marched. Travis' face

flat, pasted behind a window, an
upside down smiley
pattern behind windows tinted
khaki, his bus taking
him away from me. I leave the
dark halls, history

encased, to sit outside fortress
walls, put my head
between my knees. Gasp for
comfort. Fragile. A portrait
on my bureau at home. Acidglass
shores up the image

murlled by time. My father,
stands in sepia snow,
broad smile, eyes look beyond the
frame at me. He wouldn't have known
these boys—his age, his blood—
resisting Hitler's hand

raised, his arms against them.
Oceans, bodies of land
between my father and these
others. Here a disconnect,
a link I cannot touch or breathe.
Once I was a child

Continued

who did not have to say goodbye,
now a grandmother
who must pay the price. My
grandson. Heads for heat
and oil and sand. He, too, resists.
He, however,

unsure, doesn't know
quite why or who or what.

This Nordic rain does not, cannot wash
the memory or the present clean or clear.

Nightmare

apocalypse on the screen
at night, dreams afire.
snakes curl through a circuit
breaker

      slam of slate clouds,
      then the snap of white light,
      a musk ox dead in pasture.

wasps sense
the smell of horror, napalm.
sulfurous red
and blue flares

      low-flying copter-squitos,
      lives breathing face to face,
      slanted rainwall, death camp scrims,
      grey-wet and green.

coppola images
from another time, another
war. destruction. our national
metaphor waving proud

      slug moving along the sharp
      edge of a straight razor.
      now my grandson's computer,
      skull logo on the snap-top

arrives by Fed-Ex wearing a skin of Iraqi dust.

Freya, 1949

**Bronze sculpture by Gerhard Marcks,
German, 1889-1981**

Freya preserved in bronze,
the way Marcks

saw her in '49, a flamingo
balanced on one leg, untended

ringlets like dreadlocks, nude,
polished to a sheen, no place

to hide her secret. Freya's face,
a Zoloft tab, pregnant

triangle, Modigliani Madonna,
eyes expressionless. What made

her so? Vats of molten metal,
of course, the creative urge

but more. Arrested, the sculptor
chose her for what she has seen,

what she will not reveal
about the heat of war.

Television for Children in the Seventies

I monitored the flickering tube.
Now my daughter laments, *Sesame Street*
till I was twelve. Hodge Podge
Lodge, Captain Kangaroo,
Electric Company.
Then, "Time's up."

Not soon enough.
I watched CBS at 6 while I creamed
her tuna for toast. She knows
Kermit as well as her Mother Goose
but mostly remembers
body bags coming home.

Out of Malibu:
An American Exodus

Malibu commemorates the young son's
birth. The sculpted balsa family spends
Christmases here in a lean-to
on a bluff. A star leads others to them,
then and now.

In that time of times—no light
guided law abiding
citizens on their trek, only warm
sandy days, bitter desert nights.
No intention of becoming myth
or graven image but here they are.
A likely place to settle. Like Sinai,
familiar palms, near a sea, hard winds
weather them, still as stones,
hearts hardened to wood,
feet statue still. Exiles altered
from folk to revered. Their design
never to be worshipped, they ask
this night for compassion
and so it was.

Their feet quickened
from carvings to flesh. The choice
to stay or leave now theirs,
they travel interstate byroads
at night when they will not frighten
other sojourners, they—homeless,

Continued

shoeless, unfamiliar robes, faces
still immobile from decades
practicing the art of crèche. This new
adventure across rocky peaks, great
plains. An arch marks a river, mighty as any
they had seen, this monster land,
roads like veins, Mapquest's
blue design. As Chaucer's pilgrims sought
redemption they trudge East, leave
behind those who thought they loved
them but imposed burdens beyond
imagination, less urgency than before,
their son born, free of civic bondage.
New-turned pine aches not like ancient
flesh. In weather they had not known
earlier they walk and rest, idols
unnoticed in the snow, part of December's
pageant.

This time they follow no light
but their own, come upon an open swath,
Washington's obelisk, rotunda like Rome's,
somehow their kin, erected for the ages.
Beneath their feet the *Post,* sodden, headline
bawls *War.* Fine drizzle diffused
by starlight they stand before another,
newer wailing wall, a granite gash.

This, this! Their destination.
Rain turns to doilies (as this small

Continued

tribe turned from human tissue
to wood and back again), decorates
their cloaks, caps, hoods, slides
down the polished façade
before them. Wet-white punctuation
attach themselves to incised
names on this family's
own reflected images. They
reach to touch them,
to quench the flow.

Nations:
Tranquil Self-Destruction

"Is hero
the man missing
or man left behind
to tend the store in scorn?"

Sacred Lessons
from the *Sierra Madres*

Near a junglepath wending
to *la playa* at *Punta Monterey,*
this white fig giant.
They say Buddha
sat among its roots.
This monster tree
this lord of the slope,
once a sprout
peeked from forest desiccate,
once wrapped its tentacles
around a host, spiraled upwards,
corkscrew coils the color of ash,
once the twists widened, revealed
its ill-fated prey through keyholes,
choking, strangling.
Once an unwelcome guest
his windows seal
themselves tight. Now, now
the sole owner of this plot,
after decades, he stands,
his own tree,
roots sunk to nourish
himself.

Along comes another sapling,
pushes its tender sprout above

Continued

the moldering forest floor, leans
toward the lord.

Long years of learning
not to trust his own kind,
the lord seeps his
poisonous sap,
into the nourishment
around his roots,
he immune
but not this
youth.

Centuries beyond the giant
drops his massive body, dies,
not in the stranglehold of another
but because it is his time.

There, a gap in the canopy above
where the sky now shows blue.

Red, White, and Blue

A paradox. A gentle name like Katrina tatters
our flag, soaks it till it sags above warehouses

swimming like pork in bile. Brian and I watch
footage from CBS. He worries about interrupted

studies, grateful to be here in California's
sun feeling blue with a stranger. Together

we watch Coast Guard red copterflies
hover and dash, there a flag

painted askance from left to right
on US Chopper Number 1. Before CNN

mics, the NOPD Chief warns *This city
has been destroyed, abandoned*

by country but not by our hearts.
Troops return from badlands in one gulf

to wastelands in another where Old Miss's
antebellum past has been pummeled

to straw. We switch to Fox for lighter
fare, find futility. The *LA Times* plasters a flag

Continued

front page center—a prop starched
and stretched; inside, Kelly of Vacaville

wears an *I* ♥ *NY* shirt, adjusts
3,000 flags in memory of past

season's dead. In the *Calendar*
where one finds film and fun

Kurt Vonnegut says: ". . . look
at the 20th Century. Let's just call if off."

The Little Red Hen and Friends

Now at the fighting's
end, the busybody hen's

old friends want to peck
at the better fruits of war.

They did not plow or sow
or bring burgundy

for the stew. Today
they're keen to

share the hard-won loaf
that rose from flaccid dough,

yeasty ingredients, self-righteous grain,
to sip from that civil trough where yesterday

oil and wasted blood curled,
a paisley pattern

in cream. Fetal shapes, a membrane
on the water's surface,

reflecting salvo's
early mourning light.

Could It Have Been Otherwise?

At eighty-eight, she (tired
of the twenty first century

before it has become school
age) pleads *weary*

before dinner, eyes
too weak to read.

I turn on the TV,
grab a VCR to cheer

her. I'm too slow, way
too slow. Instead of *You're lookin'*
'

swell, Dolly, she is treated
to Aulnay-sous-Bois'

streets aflame, backlash,
ghetto or *banlieues*

nothing new.

Our Father's Flags and Ours

**With thanks to Eastwood and Speilberg's film,
*Flags of Our Fathers.***

What does hero mean?
Black, white, red or something

inbetween? Is hero the Marine
on shore or soldier

carried home, the mother
who hangs a gold banner-star

in her window for all to see
or the one who secrets sorrow

behind her door. Is hero
the man missing

or man left behind
to tend the store in scorn? Is truth

the hero or more true
the pastel lies that soften

hurting hearts? Which to honor?
One who chooses expediency

to serve the cause or he who tells truth
that sours the spirit it touches. The fabric

of firstflag hoisted more true
than the next that hangs

Continued

in memory? Colors of the original
brighter than its muddied self

the moment it was hoisted
for all to see on the horizon

or than later images of sepia
or bronze? Tattered history

sacred or new hope as scouts
raise fresh flags honoring new

lessons learned. Our flag burned asks
not for defensive postures.

In ashes martyred
it lies grander than one flown.

Devoted as he who holds his flag,
fluttering, above his head,

he draped in bunting
of red white and blue,

he who wears wristlets
or ribbons—khaki, yellow

or camouflage ruse—
is the voice

that speaks for peace.

Silence

Inspiration for this sestina was an *LA Times* report by John Daniszewski on the defacement of the new Memorial to the Victims of the Communist Terror in St. Petersburg.

Since September a monolith from Solovetsky Islands lies
against the Slavic sky. Akhmatova's incised words damn
decades of Soviet despotism have already
been despoiled with a painted swastika and David's star,
her poet's core defied, defiled once again
as it was in Communist times when she was still

alive. The stone memorializes 40,000 stilled
in Leningrad's Great Terror. The just-discovered dead lie,
where they fell, where executioners fired again
and yet again. Eleven millimeter holes are damning
evidence, radiant black stars
in the backs of skulls stained rusty red

by iron-colored clay. Now unearthed, ready
evidence tells tales of their demise. Stilled
for decades, these remains open wide their startled
eyes, unlock gaping jaws to expose lies
that men still tell, to hurl demands, to damn
those among us who deny again

caged cries hurled against
Kresty's stone walls, claims ready,
waiting to be heard anew. To thrust fingers at damned
ministers, their eyes averted, their tongues stilled,
and at society that ignores their silence and their lies.
Above Toksovo's birch groves deep night stars

Continued

light the digger's task. In fits and starts
he probes his history, stabs the fertile ground again
and again to exhume the hollow sound of lies;
his steel rod searches for truths of Stalin's time, already
known but unsubstantiated: Tens of millions stilled
in late night raids, orphans made and damned

to years of doubt, generations damned
by empty sounds of absent shame. Evidence stares
up at us from shallow graves, this field, still
today a firing range at the end of a gainless
road where a nation's defense is at the ready.
This wasted killing ground may yet lie

    mute for all the fury lying there. For when a poet's
                song is damned

    all Russia's brightest stars are doubted, the tune
              already vanquished,

    silence again imposed. Stifled voices
        cannot denounce the past.

Antigua's Hope

Sweet Potato Man sits
on the tailgate of his battered
pick-up, parked near the road
that tracks Antigua's shore
waiting for someone to pay
for his crop. Nearly black-baked
by the Carib heat as he, sweet
potatoes lie on a blanket like twists
of dark yarn.

Like a flower drawn to the sun,
Sweet Potato Man turns his face
toward traffic. Crumpled, brown
as a prune it is. Languid he is.
Waiting. His legs dangle from his perch,
limp, puppet limbs. Shoulders hunch,
sweat glints on his cheeks, his eyes
white buttons. I sense he wants
me to stop, knows

I will pass him by.

Discarded Nation

Inspired by a photograph of dying rural America by Eugene Richards published in National Geographic's January, 2008.

Frames,

neglected, their shadows
fall across snowmelt

pocked by ashfall. Abandoned
homes on North Dakota

plains, a long instant.
Huge sky

the color of gunmetal,
scrim behind a stage set,

this see-through house,
casements with no panes,

jambs with no doors, light peering
through those vacant holes.

This frame,

paint gone from slats
planks, shingles.

Frames,

cast off by families. Sad
as childhood.

The Day America Died

Historic US395. Carson City
in winter. Whistle Stop Inn
poised for demolition,
old Nugget Casino's lights
pale against the setting
sun, Heidi's Family Restaurant
celebrates its demise with balloons
red at noon, now the color of
aging blood. To the east the State's
elegant home nudged aside by a new
great granite monolith. There a spit-shine
stripcenter, Burger King.
The six o'clock news
tells us another bomb
slaughters 16.
No, now 19.

Next morning Rushbaugh condemns
free speechers
who want their soldiers home.

déjà vu

After that morning of terror
I silenced the radio, shopped

for heritage tomatoes and romaine.
Civilized decades, distant wars,

strip centers scaped with potted
palms. We forget too easily.

Nothing has changed. Really.
I reteach

myself (my young), to be alert
as badgers snouting out moles, to still

affect the serenity of a resolute monk. Peril
is not new. My ancestors beat down a scourge

of crickets with brooms, aprons, and bonnets.
Further back brandished torches fend off

carnivores that watched, waited, attacked.
Frightened as they were, they sowed, milked,

hunted, laughed around homefires. They knew
that beasts are everywhere.

The Last Curtain of Prague

The curtains in my pension
improbably are Puritan
rather than lace
from Vamberk or Brussels
or Alençon. Mornings
I'm wakened not by sounds
of the Prague Garbage Works
beneath my window,
men scurrying onto trolleys
hoisting their bristling packs,
pans, brushes, bags
to sanitize the city's past
but by these porous ghosts
that waft across my cot.
At six the free citizens walk
their pugs and Danes,
pick up and deposit
anything left behind
in canisters designated
"Psi Odpadky" so that
even doggy poop
will not contaminate
refuse of another kind.
They are on guard, these Czechs,
While I am still half-dreaming.

Utah's Song

**An excerpt from *This Is the Place*,
a novel published by AmErica House.**

Snow hums a quiet melody, rhythmic drifts,
polar staccato on cheeks and nose.
Quiet harmony here.
Solace in the pulse of canyon winds,
hush of gurgling creeks
sway of clouds moving high.
Symphony of silence
in thin mountain air.
Bars, staffs, and whole notes.
Tranquil self-destruction.

Jamaican Independence Day

Watermelons, green and yellow,
nearly round, improbably stacked
in a pyramid on the shoulder of the road,
a grass mat beneath them, no sign,
no caretaker. Busses, cars, hikers pass,
look, do not stop. But over there,
lying on a hard bench in the shade, arms
akimbo, hands a pillow behind his head,
knees tented, eyes closed, his iPod playing
an old Marley tune, the Jamaican melon man,
easy as a Sunday morning,
waits for something more.

The Story of My Missed Connection in Minneola

**A try at what poet Harry Gilleland
calls his new poetic form, a "stoerem."**

Minneola just this side of Barstow,
gas station off the freeway ramp
weathered gray, windowed dark.
decaying in the sun. My bladder
won't allow us to take the return
to I-15. Then, magically, the Minneola
Travel Store, an imitation Michigan barn, red
planks, white trim, water mumbling under a
lumber bridge. To one side two Port-A-Potties,
each with two full rolls of paper.
I had used my last Kleenex to sop up spilled
Coffee. Gratitude. Joy. Relief. I arrange the TP
into strips on the seat, push them into the pit
when I'm done, absently search for a flusher.

"We should go inside and buy something, For
having clean rest rooms," I call to my husband
through plastic walls of my odorless cell.

"Hell, we should buy something as thanks
for this place still being here," my husband
calls back, oblivious it seems to the ridiculous
aspect of communicating potty-to-potty
in the middle of nowhere.

He thinks it over."Let's skip it. Coffee's
probably been stewing for days."
We never agree.
He usually wins.
He lingers on the bridge,
finally follows me in.

Inside a rack of raccoon
hats—fake, I'm hoping. Smell
of Hazelnut Coffee. Polished Apples. Unbruised
Bananas. Whole Foods in the desert. At the back
a large, white bird picks his way along the top
of his cage, prances, like a horse trained
for dressage. He screeches, looks
at me with one eye, round, blue, a large button
pasted to smooth white facefeathers, his body by
contrast worn stubble, sallow like old stewers'
skin after my grandmother wrung their necks,
dark pinfeathers at their roots. But a beautiful
head. I hesitate. *Diseased*? I put my finger out.
He stops shrieking, puts one claw around my
forefinger as if taking the hand of a lover, then
the other, pauses, pushes his head against my
arm in a single slow motion like a cat rubbing
against its owner's leg for milk. He screams
again. I stand, stunned. The man behind me
says something I can't hear. I think the parrot
may be angry, practically throw him back
to his the perch.

Continued

The man again—large, dark unreadable
eyes—says, "He jus' wanted you to pet him."

"Oh, I misunderstood . . . " Damage
done. The parrot clings to his cage.
and I still shaking, the bird's high pitched calls
in my ears. Feeling guilty. Trying to relax, I
choose a yellow-lined pad for writing.

My husband puts his chin on my shoulder.
"Told you!"

I ask for a scoop (huge!) of Cookies and Cream
by Breyers, set them next to my husband's Diet
Coke. He's obviously still unsure of the coffee.

The man looks at my husband's cap as he gives
us change."UCLA Dad.' You a fan?"

"My daughter's a Ph.D. candidate.
So I guess . . . a fan."

"I used ta live over there."

"Westwood?" My husband's voice
is even. No trace of surprise.

"Yeah. Trouble is . . . ." The parrot screeches
again. "Quiet JoJo. The trouble is all those
ragheads moved in ya know? You can't
hardly walk down . . . "

Continued

I am uncomfortable. "Tell me, what kind of a
parrot is JoJo?"

"A Golan. Cockatoo. Thair from Indonesia.
Baretta's was diff'rent. His was from Austria—
Ost-tria. Not Os-trayyy-lia."

"My grandson's in Iraq. He loves exotic birds."

The man waves his hand above the counter.
"Hey!" A row of pink and blue bills hang there.
Scotch tape. Pushpins."Take my card. Have him
send me an Iraqi bill. And a picture of him with
a raghead. Tell im to sign it.
I'll immemorialize him."

The card says, *Jim Gallagos.* "Yeah. My middle
name's Joseph. Get it? J. J. JoJo's got my name.
M' daughters's name's
Jinny Jo. Othern's Janey Jo. Son's Jimmy Jo.
Ma gran'daughter calls me Daddy Jo.

I tell him I'll give the message
to my grandson. And I did. I told
him about JoJo but skipped the part
about the snapshot and the Iraqi bills.

Acceptance:
Waiting for the Gift

"Narcissus knows her reflection
well. She forgets to peer
under burkas, in our jails,
in the beds of the abused,
deeper, deeper into the pond . . ."

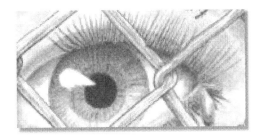

Everywhere My Dream

Rooted here, plunked among saints
until I came of age,
I followed my childman
beyond a young girl's borders
calling nowhere home,
everywhere my dream.
The Wasatch now are reverie,
salty clouds, sacraments
in puddles beneath the tires of our aging
Terraplane, sacred mountain water
in pleated cups passed
among the reverent
taken with broken bits
of Wonder bread from silver trays.
Never enough to quench
my thirst.

I sip from other waters,
the Moika—woods on the North,
on the south bank Yusupov Palace
colored like custard,
exquisite to the eyes as crème
to the tongue, the Vlatava's
furious taking of Prague,
the Hudson, New Yorkers' divide
between the nation's erudite
and anything west, as if no music
exists in Utah's *badlands*.

Continued

I do not argue. My family home,
now a vacant lot, my father gone,
Mother feeble, a snap bean waiting.
Waiting for the gift no one could
or would proffer when as children,
(my mother, holding her hands
open to cleansing cloudbursts,
then I, a generation later, wading
through cold mountain streams)
cried out to passers-by to accept
us as we were. She a bitter seed
now because she stayed,
I so lost because I went away.

The Town No One
Goes To by Accident

**With thanks to Paul Theroux who traveled back in time to
Monroeville, Alabama**

If you were to wend your way Down South
along a clay road the color of fire-bricks
after a rain, into a pineforest, cross Mush
Creek, slow down long enough to notice
anthills taller than a blood hound's tail
or lonely white churches moldered grey,
lichen like dreadlocks hanging from leafless
trees, once-upon-a-time possums now only
tell-tale teeth and crimson carcasses
picked at by crows shiny-black in early
morning sun . . .

If you were to take a timewarp trip
through Camden, Beatrice, and Tunnel Springs.
Neglected clapboards. Shotgun shacks.
Abandoned shops. Crumbling filling
stations. The church for black folk where King
shook his fist for hope.

Down that rural road a town rampant
with azaleas emerging rain-soaked
from a carpet of their own discarded petals,
matted, pale-dirty pink . . .

If you were a literary pioneer searching for a
town where folks eat turkey necks and rice
and Atticus' Old Courthouse

Continued

still stands proud, you'd find people who shrug
at the mention of *Mockingbird*
or *In Cold Blood,* a town of long
memory, a town where they sermonize
hopelessness is a bad place to be
and some say

"this town ain't no diff-rent from any other."

Auditioning for a Part

Waiting for my turn,
I speak to an Aussie.
We watch an actor
in a doctor's smock
soon to audition
for the part of a mad
scientist. Weird,
I know. But you haven't heard
Nothin' yet. My new friend
hardly notices the wild-scientist guy
pulling at his hair. She worries
that an American would grab
down the part of an Australian
reporter. She tells me
that the Geico guy on TV,
the one I can't understand
but love to watch for his googly
eyes, is really talking Cockney
and the Outback Restaurant's
pitchman is really a Kiwi.
We don't talk at all that way, she says.
I nod because I know. People take
me for a Brit and I'm from Utah,
(with a stint in New York). I'm
suddenly grateful to be in LA
in this studio where nutty people
care only about who you've become,
disdain the kind of authenticity
that doesn't count for much anyway.

Utah Child Borrows Her Song from the South

Days in mountain
shadows diminished to dark
by three.
Winter world. Sounds
in the bit-hard chill, *leg*
and *egg*, models
for Li'l Abner cartoons.
Laig and *aig*.
Round sounds like viruses
caught in noses
of those who came
before us, no rhythm,
no sweet surprises.

Foisted on me were Cockleshells,
Mrs. Pumpkin Eater imprisoned
in her shell—fare from Volume
One—when I wanted
Revere's hooves hard
on cobblestones,
and Uncle Remus' songs.

Mama (tired of trying to effect
his noise) skipped the part
where B'rer Rabbit, went
  lippity-clippity,
  clippity lippity,

Continued

only she didn't fool me. I knew
its breath. How clever those B'rers!
Because
> *B'rer Fox,*
> *he juz lay low*

and B'rer Rabbit,
that moment
familiar,
when he knocks
that tar baby silly
'cause she didn't behave
properly as he'd like.

And tar baby!
so quiet, had no name—
and she was nobody's
B'rer
> *she juz ain't*
> *sayin' nothin'.*

And now in the world
where I dream I hear
> *Mawnin'*
> *sez B'rer Rabbit,*
> *sezee,*

He as friendly as can be, the tar baby
> *she ain't suspectin''*
> *nothin'.*

Continued

These, the sounds of the South,
stay in my ears at night when I pray
and mornings when I brush,
the echoes of Remus . . .
> *sezee,*
>
> *sezee,*
>
> *sezee*

and it's lucky they do 'cause Remus'
lovely, lyrical lilt staid
in my head an no matter
who sez those stories iz right 'er thair wrong.
Thair the reason I'm gone.

Art Not Fine Enough

A sculpture by Rodin
might have been
an American icon
but a museum in Kansas
refused it. The Boston Museum
of Fine Art also refused it.
This gift offered with love,
required only crating, shipping,
and The Strength
of Conviction.
It—like his "Kiss" and "Lovers"
—he sculpted nude. Unlike
"The Kiss," this ardent
marble male
had nothing to hide
and so, it seems,
nowhere to go.

Relatives

Don't invite me back
for your turkey-dressed
up with gourmet veggies
(like creamed grapes with Brussels
sprouts) served from a silver tureen.

Don't invite me back
if you want me to nod
when your kin slaps
labels on cults and colors,
wants politicians peering
beneath my sheets, or slams
his cousin from Orange County,
who married his father's widow.

Perhaps you won't invite me back
if I mention that infamous
uncle. You know, the one who killed
three of his wives
but is candid
about who he is,
how many he's killed,
the methods he used
and never gets invited to dinner.

A Reel Left Running

Fortunate poet, born in April, your receiving
blanket laid in tender grass, your cumulous

sculpted by a breeze. Many seasons
come and gone, you lie there, watch your story

told in clouds as if projected from a reel
rolling at warp speed, your past

condensed into this moment. Outcast.
If not for *I wish you'd die so you would*

learn how wrong you are, could you know
the souls of Nora, Karinina, Hester Prynne?

Sense how you and they are one?
Without the press of mores, *good girl, chaste,*

would you look into the eyes of the Muslim,
draped, waiting for a bus in Bel Air?

If not for your imagining in liquid ink the stories
of an old man swaddled in gauze

on the corner of Broadway and 32nd, those
riding the subway without coats in December,

who might you be? Now age obscures
images, pulled taffy, whisked meringue,

Continued

they melt, struggle to be named.
So much to say, your craft

left idle for years, tools lay fallow,
and now, now there is so little time.

The Giraffe

Unaware
he was endangered,
(I unaware he might
be dangerous),
he reached for me,
barriers no match
for his neck, sniffed
my hair and with a tongue
generous as my head
kissed my face.

Olvera Street Tutorial

A command performance.
My daughter, a cultural anthropologist,
demands I take a quick ride

on our new Gold Line, from suburbs
to central LA, off at the art deco
and mission-style train station,

posing as if they were one
art form. This an adventure
from my sculpted world of silver-only

cars, little black cocktail dresses.
Kiosks call. Tacky eye treats.
Slick foil-finished ukuleles,

clay piggy banks brushed
with royal and red daisy strokes.
Faux Brighton bags and Chanel

totes hang near egg cartons
filled with tiny tin *Milagros.*
The sweet odor of *churros*

invites me to visit a cart on wheels.
I reject them, even though they're boiled
in oil thick and hot enough to suffocate

Continued

any microbe. That day
women clutch dolls, icons
with clay heads, lace crimped

and glued onto chairs in which they,
unlike babies, sit upright like T-squares
wearing folded-foil crowns set

with plastic-cut jewels. In a store
cluttered with painted tin mirrors
one girl, nearly a grown woman,

buys such a doll, unclothed. Its skin
the color of mocha latté, she runs
her finger along its arm and cheek.

She would make its garment,
stitch sequins on its satin robe,
place the tiara like a halo on painted

porcelain curls. My daughter
once crocheted a skirt of variegated
purple, an uneven hem. She wore

it with a flower more pasty
papiér maché than silk, behind her ear.
My mother hated that I let her go

to school looking like that, her panties
visible through loose stitches
her vulnerability disguised

Continued

only by cheap, looped yarn.
I revisit a booth. *Se vende*
said the sign above batiste

blouses, muslin skirts—hand-crocheted,
too—red and blue yarn fix orange
ruffles to purple. I admire

the colors like paper placemats
crayoned by toddlers. I drink
a *horchata,* ricey-sweet, taste

a triangle of watermelon offered by
a boy sitting on a curb near
the *Mission Nuestra Señora Reine.* He cuts

another: I notice juice trails
from his sticky penknife to his elbow
and eat it anyway. I try a straw hat;

its brim blooms with crépe paper poppies,
bright as this Mexican street. Perhaps next visit
I shall buy one and wear it the entire day.

Whiling Summer's Hours

August's tedium. I search
for four leafs among clover,
imagine lucky shamrocks,
scoop pollen from the stamens
of hollyhocks that grew wild
along the barbed wire fences,
collect four-o-clock seeds
the shape of hand grenades
in my uncle's duffle
when he returned from Iwo Jima,
listen to the hum of bees caught,
lid to lip, in a Kerr canning jar.
Sometimes I let them go
when the sides were dim
with the wet of their effort,
                      sometimes not.

With time left over
I pinched the legs
from grasshoppers,
watched them spit
tobacco, their mandibles
working like fingers
massaging sourdough.

Continued

Then pulled off
parts that whirred,
spread out their filaments
to collect their yellow
in the light, admire veins,
pretend they were wings
                              of butterflies.

Woman to Woman

The women in these parts. Ancient.
Twisted like *krumholz* near the treeline.
This one, the keeper of the cemetery,

hunches against the perpetual gale,
Antarctic plague that has not ceased
from Magellan's time to this.

Even in this hemisphere's
summer sun, she shrivels,
a desiccated leaf, mentions

how beautiful their flowers,
wind-worn petunias on the graves.
I tuck the label on my handbag

under my arm, pull gloves
over cruise-manicured nails,
tell myself it is the southern chill.

Fingernails like bark, she points
to the tomb of the unknown
Indian boy, Punta Arenas' saint,

savior of sick children, reaches
to stroke his bronze hand. Women
believe in his touch, *una plegaria.*

Continued

Hundreds of plaques nailed there,
thanking him. *Milagro de milagros.*
A child is saved. The keeper

of the cemetery smiles, teeth
like stumps, eyes soft, accepting.
She seems to know I understand.

The Way Poppies Were

Poppies before Belgium
borrowed them, pinned
them to lapels, reminders
of their fields
of dead.
Before Afghanistan,
ghettoes or halfway houses.

Poppies along trails
I walked, nodding in a breeze.

Poppies picked on summer
days, upended to join my hollyhock
parade of dancing ladies dressed
in dainty pink and white, these new
revelers in carnival-red ballgowns,
snapdragon heads attached
with toothpicks, crimson-confetti
rose petals scattered
along their route.

Poppy petals bold, plucked
as if tender daisies. Does he love
me, does he not.

Poppies blinking black eyes.

Continued

Poppies shed their gowns,
now pot-bellied pods open,
pepper our garden with sooty

seeds, full of life, those seeds
Mother sprinkled on Parker House
rolls after she'd rolled them, pinched
them, brushed them with egg white.

Poppy pods now miniature monks
with black tonsures,
rather than dancing girls, they now
circled with crowns of thorns
like Jesus wore to Calvary.

Ypres' Jewish Grave

There may have been more marked
with David's Star but this grave, unstained
in 80 years, stones, perched atop
its arch makes me think of another grave

near Terezin, a sight I'd never then seen.
Beneath a sycamore piles of pebbles
commemorate what had been given there,
and taken.

Now this at Tynecot, unexpected
as then but familiar. Skies the color
of dry-docked ships. Spade-turned trenches
of loam join monument to monument,

tenuous plants tamped to greet
the coming spring, not an unkempt
clot or rock in sight. The Belgians flooded
their homeland against invaders, water their best

soldier, their magic defender, passive perhaps
but nonetheless bold defiance. This grave kin
to that action, unique slab among thousands,
its palm-sized pebbles materialized. Like the

floods they make liars of those who say they
didn't serve.

outlier

my heart an exile, cast
from my homeland,
banished from my cradle,
my pallid face an émigré
silent, solitary.

my book a pariah,
an exoskeleton beside
other covers other spines.
it pastels beside
titles stamped by
prodigy presses.

my designation obscure,
a vivid pebble submerged
in a great tide, a tack upon
a sandy beach. i gasp, cry out.
literate tribes
do not hear my voice.

A Revisionist View:
What Life Given for Chess?

Blood sacrifice for tusk of elephant
ambered like aging teeth for this set carved.
Eyes and fingers drained in the delving
and scraping required to decorate the pieces
with delicate beads, tassels, pikes, turbans,
shields. Also those who inspired
the game, pawns of confronting armies,
dead.

Terezin Fresco

Written during my visit to the Terezin Detention Camp Memorial in the Czech Republic.

Crystal memories

Fragmented shards

Cleansed scraps

Congealed into

Stucco tears.

LÖWNER THOMAS

Child of terror

Born in April

Like me.

On the fourth

Like me.

1935

I am 60.

He is never.

White Girl Says Goodbye to a Fleeting Love In Front of Her Mother

Why would I
want
this young Masai,
soon-chief,
a Kenyan Kobe,
teeth glare-white
in equator sun,
his royal staff
glints, his robe the color
of the Chalbi in flower.
Noon heat,
flies hum in our ears,
faces, noses. The smell
of cow dung wattle.

Why would he
want
me? On the horizon
his young wives
display their tribal
dance, each a spring
coiled, then a jump,
long slender legs,
straight-armed
to see beyond their
boundaries?

Continued

Still he touches the curve
of my silver cell,
my shoulder, there
near my tank strap.

Now the sky dark
velvet. We say goodbye.
Fire, embers like Kenya's
billion flies, soar
toward the stars,
reach for their light.
Something more
embodied than hope.
Smoke fills our eyes
with tears.

The Boy on an American Flight

He screws open his Oreo,
licks the cream clean,
puts one Nike on the seat
before him and pushes,
then turns wide, dark eyes
on me from across
the aisle and grins. I only know
he is Muslim because his
mother wears a *hijab*.

a little tiff

debate, dispute, bicker,
squabble, wrangle, riled,
argue, angry-as-hell, fuming,
furious, irate, livid, infuriated,
incensed, enraged, totally
pissed off. Today my mother
decided to live, played
the Prodigal Son Game,
(only it was an updated
version—a preference for son
over daughter) and I learned
to call a spat a spat, an argument
a fight-to-the-death.

Oh, how I learned
that I am not the sweet little
poet-girl everyone thinks me,
                        most of all me.

Great Equalizer

In a suit of nubs and braid,
silk stockings, Prada pumps,

a woman's body bends forward,
better to be heard. Traffic.

Construction. Another, potato woman,
starched collar and cuffs, plastic

nametag on her bosom. New York's
odd couple. In the shade of Wall

Street's Exchange, Miss Chanel,
with her Tiparillo,

Señora Brooklyn her Salem.

Acceptance

Georgia's soft song
calls
    pale cobwebs
    from my mind.
I curl into the palm of distant decades
    gentle hands
    muted manners
lidded eyes
subtle smiles
caring questions:
    "Do you believe?"
    "Do you accept?"
    "Are you saved?"
  an assonant arsenal
    soft syllables,
    determined clubs
      silence my soul.

Nothing I Can Do

Boots on the ground. Tough
message. That and *surge.*

My grandson—gentle
reader of Hemingway, Steinbeck,

E.B. White—wears cowboy-American
boots. In my dream Charlotte

sends Templeton off to find
the perfect phrase to save

Travis with her web of words,
that magic combination

that makes her growing audience
see in her dewy message

what they hadn't seen before. The rat,
suddenly eager for the task,

snuffles through cotton-candy smeared
refuse, brings back a torn clipping

for all who come to worship
at Charlotte's silk alter. It says

boots in sinking sand.

Escape

My father didn't die,
the woman says.
He escaped.

She sits, hand in lap, bruised blue letters in
the web between her thumb and forefinger,
her huge Hungarian eyes hungry
and hurried.

I think: death, detainee, concentration,
the plagues of her race and decade.
But no, she speaks instead of disapproval,
disparagement, desecration, denigration,
superstition, malicious scorn. From her
aunt's, sisters' and mother's mouths.

Another world's hurt creeps up her throat,
a rash of ruined hopes.
Generations of pain pool in her eyes,
hollow shaded-trails of blue beneath them.
Censure's sting chords
the sound she makes
like sputtering electric filaments.

The Power of Pickaninny

My pickaninny doll, her black
nappy crimps tied up in ribbons,
a porcupine-do much like my own nighttime
gear. The doll's red grosgrain,
tight-tied to tame her curls; mine white
rags torn from old sheets
lumpy on my head for the sake
of ringlets.

Henna for shine, lemon
for light, home perms for curls,
I the model, Mama the sculptor,
until I could not gasp enough air,
a brown paper bag balloon—breathe
in, breathe out—to keep
the room from swirling dark
like my life consumed down
the maelstrom in the bathtub drain.
Later I choose brush rollers
for body—each a hedgehog—pricks
my scalp as I sleep but this discomfort
I foist on myself for beauty's sake.

> Now I let my hair go silver,
> cut it for comfort, spurn platform
> shoes and Weight Watchers, accept
> lipstick the color of raspberries. Or not.

Continued

I touch the soft
hide of a snake without fear,
know what I didn't notice
then, that Pickaninny was black,
I white, wordpower packed
by purpose, its sound as it's meant,
not its collection of letters.
Pickaninny and I. Hair,
—pulled-pain—make us one.

Narcissus Revisited

Wish not but work. We need
more than what we have.
Let us be measured
not for height or at the hip
but for the our roles.
Compensate us for compassion
so we might look beyond
our foyers with that rare
and precious skill.

I may not want,

> but many of my kind do. Women.
> Hidden, squeezed, ignored, ridiculed,
> manipulated, raped, murdered.
> Pain, poverty, politics. All enemies
> dark shadows, seaweed undulating
> beneath the sheen

of the life I live.

> Even when I gaze deep
> and recognize the algae
> there, feel their vile shapes,
> I do not recognize hubris,
> lurking among them, women's
> worst foe. Those who feel

Continued

new freedoms like I, some later-borns
unaware that they are new, accept
the yellow-bright shimmer
spread across the surface
as if it were our doing or our due.
Acceptance works best
when paired with gratitude.

Why then do we forget
what others did for us,
what there is yet to do?

Narcissus knows her reflection
well. She forgets to peer
under burkas, in our jails,
in the beds of the abused,
deeper, deeper into the pond
beneath, where some
            still suffocate.

From the Observation Deck

A stranger. His hand shields his eyes
to see the beach from here.
His face pushes into a grin,
smile tracks at the corners
of his eyes, along his cheekbones
like those that play
in my makeup mirror.
I don't mind his at all.
A young woman, white and slender
as the egret on the shore
comes to fetch him. His face
relaxes; radiating lines
from lid to temples ebb
like waves on sand, creases
now streaks of white drawn
with chalk on tanning
hide, squint lines never colored
by the sun. They shout his age.
I frown, feel the crinkles between
my brows. His lady seems not to see
his, nor does she seem to care.

This Fragile Art of Warfare

In my dreams. The Chinese
call it clouds and rain,
this delicate tingling
art, restraint intensifies pleasure.
Like a bow brought taught,
a kind of warfare this love,
waiting, waiting for the moment exquisite.
                                    Without flint
or force, only your whisper,
your gentle touch.
Tender persuasion.
To make me want your way.

Forging Ski Trails

Newwoman pushes weights,
manages moguls. I, the blurred
outer edge of her generation

glimpsed, molded her sunlit tracks
with the steel edges of my Rosignols.
Now I ski but forsake diamonds

for bunny hills, max at four
runs. Still, I am her filament
to the future, stretched

like spun glass. A new career
at 60, rejuvenated marriage (orgasmic
subtext) and there, over the ridge at 70!

Walks at dusk, a hot toddy in the lodge.
Perhaps I'll write a poem to be memorized
by those who follow.

Background Singers

We the girl singers.
Twenty steps they said was all it takes
to front and center, circle of silver,
cause we got what it takes—any one of us—
has a voice we'd like to be heard.
We th' girl singers
know our worth, blended
black—R&B, gospel,
zydeco, sweet deep throats
and *blursounds, humthrums*
straight out of Harlem
jazz clubs.

We the dirty little secret
big stars' successes ride
on. We th' hit makers,
our *sh-sh-shoos, ring-a-ling-dings*.
We the sexy legs, boobs, butts,
the raw notes
that sell discs for white boys,
Sting, Mick. And black ones, too.
We give Charles, even the King
of Pop their pizzazz.
We know it.
They know it.
They admit it.

Continued

Some of us never wanted more
but for those who did, those twenty
feet to the footlights
were a trek. Fanny pats, all-night gigs,
catching buses with scummed
windows and tacky gum
in the aisles when the whole of LA's
stretching their bones
to get out of bed for the day, desperately
mopping other women's floors by sunlight.
Taking shit from Schlecters
of the world, the Ike Turners—
and marrying 'em did no good
neither.

We who wanted the spotlight
standing there in sweet, pink
smoke, we the rebels.
We the believers. We the ones raised
on *The Lord lift us up where we belong.*
We activists, th' ones who laid
aside our principles for *Sweet Home Alabama*
cause we paid the price *b-ba-bab-ee.*
We the ones who do not what *you* want
but what *I do.*
We the ones who sing 'bout sex
when no one admits that's what we're singin'

Continued

and we the ones who do it
with a red dress on.

"I always thought if I gave my heart
I'd be a star."
Yeah, yeah, yeah.

Healing

A man and woman, together
Across the waiting room
Healing touch, hand to knee.
His body bowed and bumpy
Like a snap bean.
Her frame bent like her cane,
Her feet slow and flat, eyes glossy.
She limps from him, drawing her fingers
Across his open hand.
He watches her until she is gone.
"Why dint they play cards on th' ark?"
His voice large in the quiet,
Magazines, faded and creased,
Children's beads and building blocks.
"Because Noah sat on th' deck."
"Would you like t' hear another?"
"What kind of light did he have on th' ark?"
The receptionist's vacant voice answers
politely. A young man nudges
his other, eyes lowered to the slats of
calm winter sun on the carpet.
"A floodlight."
There is no answer.
"How did th' pioneers pay fer their food?"
I wait. Finally, a curative question.
"Tell me," I say.

Continued

115

"They used winter quarters."
"What did they think of th' crickets?"
"They thought they were for th' birds."

A white coat moves through the room.
"Mr. Hanson, we can't help your…."

"Why don't they have telephones in China?

"Why?"

"They are afraid they'll wing th' wrong Wong."

"Mr. Hanson…
The woman returns, sandpiper legs
Step-stepping on sand.
"Give me another riddle, Hon,"
She teeters, reaches out.

"UPS merged with Fed Ex. What did they call it?"

She takes a cane from him, his palm over
her veined, palsied hand.
They laugh.
"Fed-Up?" she says.

Consensus, Censorship, Expectations

Radio hosts never ask you
about the point of *his* shoe
or the cut of *his* lapel. Probably
just as well. You might say
something about kicking ass
with a well-placed sole
rather than a toe.
Only worse. You—polite sweet
you—might make a point
about how price tags
aren't necessarily
a reflection of class.
And come to regret it.

Death by Ferris Wheel

From her seat in the gondola a woman
who might be me watches roller

bladers with supple bones, toddlers with careless
balloons far, far down on the pier. She opens

the doors—mini saloon doors of purple—
or she crawls over acrylic barriers. Either way

she hesitates a moment. The lurch
of the wheel as it stops at the top finishes

the job. No scream. A plane floating a campaign
trail of plastic behind, silent. Soundless

waves, too, that far up. She floats as if posing
for her close-up, delicate fingers, poised toes,

her red sunhat a Frisbee against
sky of pulled taffy clouds on blue.

Sea like scallops of Alençon lace below,
sand stretched away toward the Palisades,

the smell of sugary *churros* her last sensation.

Future:
Stones of Distrust

"I like best the poems of Ahkhmatova
that recount repression for they always
(I believe in "always")
are indelible, like simple joys. . ."

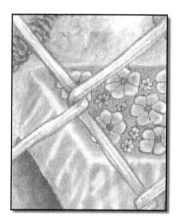

Population Dying

My people live, the
ones for whom ancient
will someday fit, drinking clean,

working hard, now casualties
of war that never was. My nonstop
to LA banks away from the Wasatch.

I am struck by souls,
the ones I know—and the ones
I don't—invisible from 20,000 feet

like the radium in their veins and mine.
Little can now be done. My husband's
examination was fine. Strong heart, lungs

but blood poisoned,
when fear, the hardest,
coldest warrior—was foisted

on us. We desert people were nothing
to the those who wasted Nevada's
sand, planned that western

winds would cool our faces in August's
heat, denied that they would plant
tumorseeds, and decades later,

for those of us who pause to consider,
                              stones of distrust.

Falkland's Town Crier

From his home Mike Butcher makes his point.
His town is Leg-O-Land, red roofs like plastic

bricks, peat sod walls separate green Monopoly
houses from brick hotels. Beyond, Stanley

harbor idles, a mirror, Falkland's connection
to the world. Near Pioneer Road, Mike's gate—

a Magellenic penguin, iron-wrought—does not
invite me in. No need, really. Rusty

cannon so close I could touch
it through the fence, its voice

a hand-scrawled sign, *22,000 lives it took
from '37 to '65.* Remnants of its deeds pock

his yard. Over there beside Mike's potato patch,
a Minke jaw, farther on a sperm whale's spine,

here harpoon clusters like arrows
that emblem-eagles clasp in their talons

bound with explosives
to assure their spurs wreak instant death.

We needn't chat over tea, Mike and I.

Sticking in My Craw

Voracious cells dined on my womb.
  Nourished by cow's meal
  doped for growth, penicillin
  pumped into fouls' flesh. Now I refuse
  sweet sizzle, pungent
  char-spices beckoning
  from the grill. One day
  I succumb, hold a morsel
  to my mouth, recoil. It is not about my
  life
  but its.
  Unspeakable lunch.

Indelible

I like best the poems of Ahkhmatova
that recount repression for they always
(for I believe in "always")
are indelible, like simple joys—turtles,
bees, and clouds—confirm
survival.
However invisible
that confirmation
may seem.

Gulping Oxygen

The water cooler, ungainly.
irrelevant gasps

for air, bursts bright
as soap bubbles, quick

as magic tricks, urgent gusts.
Secrets. Needs. If only

someone would pause,
to see the beauty there

or at least to listen
to its call for help.

Sounds of Seasons

I imagine sounds of the seasons in color,
no chiaroscuro dreams for me, no measuring

the earth's turning by clocks, quarters,
segments or three month intervals. Time

a running board straight from here onward,
no end at winter or waning life but a cycle

beyond 70 or 80 or death. *Time* says at 88
Krikorian toys with GM, nothing more

than his Rubric cube. His business. His life.
He knows no seasons, validates my dream.

Work forever, or work to live without end,
whichever comes first. Engines gun,

tires slap asphalt, faster, faster than the limit and
colors. Tulips. Magenta, licorice red, ecstasy

white, solar bursts, flares yellow-hot. Now—
wherever, whenever now is—we point our toes

at the pedal and accelerate. Beyond light, color
and seasons. I am not afraid. I have the time

to do what I do.

Rosa Parks Memorialized

On the day our September losses
reached 2,000, a tribute
to Rosa. If she were alive
now, vital in her fourth decade,
what would she say about
intolerance in its newer habit?
Could her voice
make a difference now,
now! So many ears to reach,
so many ways to reach them,
so determined in righteousness
they are? No matter
how tuned, would her solo
be enough or do we need
now a choir singing,
thousands screaming
shrill at once?
Come to think of it,
that was required then, too. Elegant.
Gentle. Firm. But not
enough without the rest of us.

Unraveling Star Wars

She pulls putty from her keyboard,
unravels universal taffy. K.C. Cole
must be quick about it, for natural
forces doom space, time

and us. She my Princess
Leia (smart, firm, stable) untangles
millenniums with her words
so we, seduced by nature's face,

might see the magician's slight
of hand, ruses, mistakes—stretched,
warped, shrink-wrapped.
We, willing to believe,

perch here in swaths
of space, hang on quantum
mechanics when other beliefs
falter,

even when new ideas make
no more sense than old
ones. We—absurd—know our importance
but Cole lets us understand

we are sherds learning Einstein's
leftovers, all our moments
(and his)
everpresent.

Continued

A letter from New York whispers
snow is falling now.
Now, now, now.
Here in LA? New York?
Then? Now? No need. Each moment

exists somewhere, sometime in space
and snow? Snow I know, is real now
and then, there and even here
where snow has never fallen.

We see. We note. We pin it down.
That's the magic.
It's the poet and the poetry.
The poet observes, describes

how the universe survives
and doesn't. How it's as good
as it gets. Eggs
don't unscramble. Physics

doesn't tell time
or which way to go. The big bang
does that. Out, out, hidden
power greater

than the cosmos, out
into an impossibly ordered
state that reveals—somehow—the great
conjurer.

Continued

Soon what we know
(and don't know) will squander
its beauty if Planetwars or Starwars
don't destroy it first or if our

Magicwoman
doesn't fix things (or already has)
before we annihilate
Higgs's loaf of warm bread.

Sifting Out Life's Dregs

I embrace that number, miraculous,
though I can't say when or which

it was. The year five candles propped
in butter cream indicated decades? Later

when sixty blazes demanded
a sheet cake—flourless—to support

the weight? Or was it a lucky digit
nestled within those decades?

Whenever. That number (or the krinkles
around my eyes) became a filter, pure

as linen paper cups tucked
in my Coffeemaster where little

intolerant, bigoted, impatient
uncaring seeps into the liquid of my life

but allows surprises still. A young student
I met in Prague who cares only for heart,

a child who has not (yet?) learned
about barriers, an ancient who doesn't count

passing years. Each an addition to the mix—salt,
nutmeg—lose their grit, dissolve into days,

Continued

flavor them each fresh, immeasurable.
Like Bleached Perfection Flour sifting

into an aqua bowl softer than it began,
my time gets better. Deer chomping

backyard roses, beauty eating beauty. I share
my lavender and blue-black petals

with them willingly as the common
link, hear larks above traffic's

buzz. Age is the beginning.
We do whatever it takes. Kiss,

marry, order extra candied
walnuts for our salads

Interpreting Fairy Tales

Orchids
for Mother's Day.
Tiny Thumbelinas
on long-legged stems,
innocent dancing-down-dillies
in yellow petticoats,
so tiny I don't see
their parts, ovaries
open to bees
and hummer-commers,
delicate vulvas,
pink-painted sepals.

Forty years ago a young
man, now my husband,
brings a corsage,
not a gardenia
pungent, bruised,
like other girls'
but a single orchid,
green.

I, so young! Don't know
papillae, nectar,
fleshy inner parts
only how pretty pinned
to my breast.
I don't think
green,

Continued

virginal. The two of us,
              soon to germinate.

From That to This,
the connection.
How what I didn't know
and how the knowing
changes things. Riotous
orchids, baa baa black sheep,
ugly ducklings. Here, a single
troll waits under a bridge.
His name is Time.

About the Author

Carolyn Howard-Johnson

Carolyn Howard-Johnson's poetry reflects her background in journalism. Her style owes much to her mentor Suzanne Lummis (star poetry instructor for UCLA Extension's Writers' Program) and by extension former US poet laureate Phillip Levine who was known for a straight forward style known as the Fresno School of Poetry. That school is down-to-earth— often with a nitty gritty edge—but more importantly, as least as far as Carolyn is concerned, the ability to find complete sentences across line breaks.

Carolyn's several careers prepared her for promoting her own books and those of others. She was the youngest person ever hired as a staff writer for the *Salt Lake Tribune*—"A Great Pulitzer Prize Winning Newspaper"— where she wrote features for the society page and a column under the name of Debra Paige. That gave her insight into the needs of editors, the very people authors must work with to get free ink. Being familiar with the way news is handled helps her see how different books—even poetry— fit into different news cycles.

Later, in New York, she was an editorial assistant at *Good Housekeeping Magazine*. She also handled accounts for star fashion publicist Eleanor Lambert who instituted the first Ten Best Dressed List. Writing releases for celebrity designers of the day including Pauline Trigere, Rudy Gernreich, and Christian Dior required an eye for color and form. Those same skills were needed when she helped produce photo shoots for Lambert's clients . . . and later as a poet.

Carolyn's experience in journalism and as a poet and author of fiction and nonfiction helped the multi award-winning author understand how different genres can be marketed more effectively. She was an instructor for UCLA Extension's renowned Writers' Program for nearly a decade and has studied writing at Cambridge University, United Kingdom; Herzen University in St. Petersburg, Russia; and Charles University in Prague. She worked as columnist, reviewer, and staff writer for the *Pasadena Star-News*, *Home Décor Buyer*, the *Glendale News-Press* (an affiliate of the *LA Times*), Myshelf.com, and others.

Her HowToDoItFrugally series of books for writers are all multi award-winners and her marketing campaign for the second book in that series, *The Frugal Editor*, won the Next Generation Indie Best Book Award for marketing as well as coveted awards from USA Book News, Global E-book Awards, the Irwin Award, and others. She also has a multi award-winning series of HowToDoItFrugally books for retailers.

Howard-Johnson was honored as Woman of the Year in Arts and Entertainment by California Legislature members Carol Liu, Dario Frommer, and Jack Scott. She received her community's Character and Ethics award for her work promoting tolerance with her writing and the Diamond Award in Arts and Culture from her community's Library and Arts and Culture Commissions. She was named to *Pasadena Weekly's* list of "Fourteen Women of the San Gabriel Valley Who Make Life Happen" and Delta Gamma, a national fraternity of women, honored her with their Oxford Award.

Carolyn is an actor who has appeared in ads for Apple, Lenscrafters, Time-Life CDs, Marlboro, Blue Shield, Disney Cruises (Japan) and others. She admits to being an English major in college but denies preferring diagramming sentences to reading a good daily newspaper.

Her Web site is HowToDoItFrugally.com. She blogs writers resources at Writer's Digest's 101 Best Websites pick SharingwithWriters.blogspot.com and rants about wordiness and grammar issues at The Frugal, Smart, and Tuned-In Editor blog, TheFrugalEditor.blogspot.com.

About the Artist

Richard Conway Jackson

 Richard Conway Jackson is serving twenty-five years to life for receiving stolen property in California. His days are filled with drawing and writing, some published in literary magazines. His art is catalogued by CHI-EY INC that publishes print-on-demand greeting cards using prisoners' franchised art. His work was also published in an issue of *Rebel Rodz* magazine and two poetry books: *Swallow* (Amsterdam Press, 2009) and *Barbie at 50* (Cervena Barva Press, 2010), by Jendi Reiter.

The artist is waiting for Recall of Sentence proceedings in Los Angeles Superior Court. In 2015 he will have spent twenty-one years in California State prisons.

"Carolyn Howard-Johnson is like three poets plus two writers all wrapped into one." ~Suzanne Lummis, poetry instructor for UCLA Extension Writers' Program and honored Los Angeles poet.

Tracings: A Chapbook of Poetry
Published by Finishing Line Press
Awards: Award of Excellence from Military Writers Society of America, Compulsive Readers Ten Best Reads
ISBN: 1-59924-017-3
To order paperback or e-book on Amazon: bit.ly/CarolynsTracings

Tracings touches chords—both major and minor—for readers interested in nostalgia, tolerance, culture, and aging. The author traces her life's experiences and for her it feels like "a movie reel running backwards."

-∞-

Celebration Series
Coauthored with Magdalena Ball

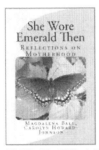

She Wore Emerald Then: Reflections on Motherhood
Coauthored by Carolyn Howard-Johnson and Magdalena Ball
Self-published in the fine tradition of poets everywhere
Awards: USA Book News finalist for poetry, Military Writers Society of America honorable mention

ISBN 13: 978-1438263793
ASIN: B00BXPW2XO
To order paperback or e-book on Amazon:
bit.ly/MothersChapbook

"[Both] poets continue to write poems that don't sound either like banal Hallmark cards or the bitter-at-dysfunctional-family jeremiads that habitually torture MFA writing workshop participants."
~Kristin Johnson, screenwriter and founder of the Warrior Poets Project

-∞-

Cherished Pulse:
A Chapbook of Unsyrupy
Love Poetry
Coauthored by Carolyn Howard-Johnson
and Magdalena Ball
Artwork by Vicki Thomas
Self-published in the fine tradition of
poets everywhere
Awards: USA Book News finalist for poetry
ISBN 13: 978-1438263793
To order paperback or e-book on Amazon:
bit.ly/CherishedPulse

". . . snapshots of love by two gifted poets."
~ Willie Elliott for MyShelf.com

-∞-

Imagining the Future:
Ruminations on Fathers and Other
Masculine Apparitions

Coauthored by Carolyn Howard-Johnson and Magdalena
Ball
Self-published in the fine tradition of poets everywhere
ISBN: 144997774X
To order paperback or e-book on Amazon:
bit.ly/Imagining

"[Both poets] have an incredible gift with literary imagery."
~ Darcia Helle

-∞-

Blooming Red:
Christmas Poetry for the Rational

Coauthored by Carolyn Howard-Johnson and Magdalena Ball
Artwork by Vicki Thomas
Self-published in the fine tradition of poets everywhere
Awards: USA Book News finalist, Silver Award from Military Writers' Society of America
ISBN: 9781449948245
To order paperback or e-book on Amazon: bit.ly/BloomingRed

-∞-

Deeper into the Pond:
A Celebration of Femininity

Coauthored by Carolyn Howard-Johnson and Magdalena Ball
Artwork by Jacquie Schmall
Award: Bronze medal from Military Writers' Society of America
Self-published in the fine tradition of poets everywhere
ISBN: 978146115934
To order paperback or e-book on Amazon: bit.ly/DeeperPond

"Whatever your age these poems will speak to you of times to look forward to or to remember. These are not poems to be read once. They will stay with you forever."
~ Nancy Famolari, author.

-∞-

Sublime Planet:
Honoring Earth Day for the World and Universe

As Featured in the Earth Day Issue of
The Pasadena Weekly

Coauthored by Carolyn Howard-Johnson and Magdalena Ball
Photography by Ann Howley
Awards: Finalist USA Book News 2013
ISBN: 9781482054705
ASIN: B000BRLF5GA
To order paperback or e-book on Amazon: amzn.to/SublimePlanet
Proceeds from *Sublime Planet* go to World Wildlife Fund

"Lucid and erudite." ~ Midwest Book Review

POETRY TEXT
Master Class Poetry Mystique: Inside the Contemporary Poetry Workshop

Edited and commentary by Suzanne Lummis, ©2014. A text on the writing process. Featuring poems by Suzanne's students
Available in paperback on Amazon: bit.ly/SuzanneLummis

–∞–

About Carolyn's Other Literary Works

This is the Place

AmErica House
Awards: Eight awards
Published by AmErica House
Out of print, but available using Amazon's new and used feature
ISBN: 1588513521
To order used in paperback:
bit.ly/ThisIsthePlace

"Howard-Johnson strengthens her novel with behind-the-scenes details of Mormon life and history in a book suitable for all collections, particularly those where . . . Orson Scott Card's religious books are popular."
~ *Library Journal*

-∞-

Harkening: A Collection of Stories Remembered

AmErica House
Awards: Three awards including Word Thunder's Excellence in Writing award
Out of print. Available using Amazon's new and used feature
ISBN: 1591295505
To order used in paperback:
bit.ly/TrueShortStories

". . . a magnificent writer . . .timeless and universal ."
~ Rolf Gompertz, author of *Abraham, the Dreamer: An Erotic and Sacred Love Story*

Forthcoming Books

Here's How I Don't Cook: A Memoir

Being shopped by Agent Terrie Wolf
Webpage on Carolyn's site:
howtodoitfrugally.com/heres_how_i_dont_cook.htm

> "[After rereading] once again I've decided *Here's How I Don't Cook* is my favorite memoir. ~ Terrie Wolf, Agent, AKA Literary Management

-∞-

This Land Divided

Being shopped by Agent Terrie Wolf

The great Mormon-American novel.
~ K Ventrice

**For more information,
interviews or blog material contact
hojonews@aol.com**

Made in the USA
San Bernardino, CA
30 January 2016